Coyotes

Kit Caudron-Robinson

Explore other books at:
WWW.ENGAGEBOOKS.COM

VANCOUVER, B.C.

WWW.ENGAGEBOOKS.COM

Coyotes: Level 3
Animals That Make a Difference!
Caudron-Robinson, Kit,
Text © 2023 Engage Books
Design © 2023 Engage Books

Edited by: A.R. Roumanis, Melody Sun,
and Ashley Lee
Design by: Mandy Christiansen

Text set in Arial Regular.
Chapter headings set in Nathaniel-19.

FIRST EDITION / FIRST PRINTING

All rights reserved. No part of this book may be stored in a retrieval system, reproduced or transmitted in any form or by any other means without written permission from the publisher or a licence from the Canadian Copyright Licensing Agency. Critics and reviewers may quote brief passages in connection with a review or critical article in any media.

Every reasonable effort has been made to contact the copyright holders of all material reproduced in this book. Image on page 9 by James Gayaldo.

LIBRARY AND ARCHIVES CANADA CATALOGUING IN PUBLICATION

Title: Coyotes / Kit Caudron-Robinson.
Names: Caudron-Robinson, Kit, author.
Description: Series statement: Animals that make a difference

Identifiers: Canadiana (print) 20230448542 | Canadiana (ebook) 20230448569
ISBN 978-1-77476-832-7 (hardcover)
ISBN 978-1-77476-833-4 (softcover)
ISBN 978-1-77476-834-1 (epub)
ISBN 978-1-77476-835-8 (pdf)
ISBN 978-1-77878-135-3 (audio)

Subjects:
LCSH: Coyotes—Juvenile literature.
LCSH: Human-animal relationships—Juvenile literature.

Classification: LCC QL737.P94 C38 2023 | DDC J599.885—DC23

This project has been made possible in part by the Government of Canada.

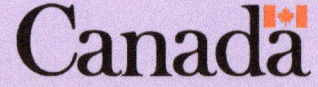

Contents

- 4 What Are Coyotes?
- 6 A Closer Look
- 8 Where Do Coyotes Live?
- 10 What Do Coyotes Eat?
- 12 How Do Coyotes Talk to Each Other?
- 14 Coyote Life Cycle
- 16 Curious Facts About Coyotes
- 18 Kinds of Coyotes
- 20 How Coyotes Help Other Animals
- 22 How Coyotes Help Earth
- 24 How Coyotes Help Humans
- 26 Coyotes in Danger
- 28 How to Help Coyotes
- 30 Quiz

What Are Coyotes?

Coyotes are mammals. Mammals are animals with warm blood and bones in their backs. Coyotes are part of the dog family.

Coyotes are often active during the day. They can be **nocturnal** when they live close to people. They do this to avoid contact with humans.

KEY WORD

Nocturnal: active at night.

A group of coyotes is called a pack.

A Closer Look

Fully grown coyotes are usually 3.3 to 4.3 feet (1 to 1.3 meters) long. They weigh 20 to 50 pounds (9 to 23 kilograms). Coyotes' coats are usually light gray or red. Some coyotes have long, thick hair.

Coyotes have a long tail. The very end of their tail is black.

Coyotes have yellow eyes that help them see at night.

Coyotes have large, sharp teeth. They use them to catch food.

Where Do Coyotes Live?

Coyotes live in deserts, mountains, prairies, and forests. They are very good at **adapting** to new surroundings. In cities, they live in green spaces. These can be places like parks, forests, or golf courses.

KEY WORD

Adapting: changing behavior in order to survive in a new environment.

Coyotes can only be found in North America. Mountain coyotes are found between British Columbia, Canada, and California in the United States. The northwest coast coyote lives west of the Cascade Range in Oregon and Washington.

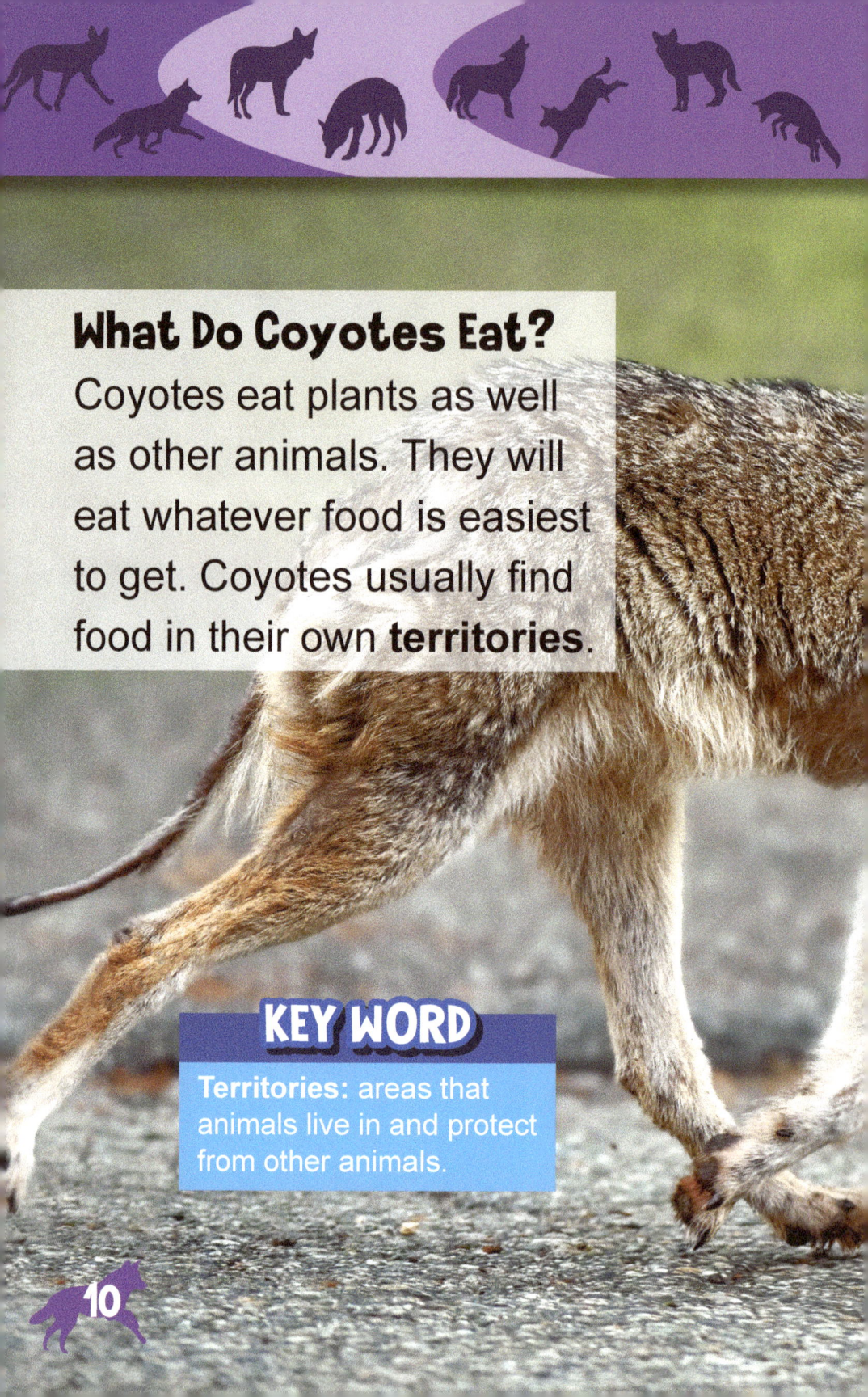

What Do Coyotes Eat?

Coyotes eat plants as well as other animals. They will eat whatever food is easiest to get. Coyotes usually find food in their own **territories**.

KEY WORD

Territories: areas that animals live in and protect from other animals.

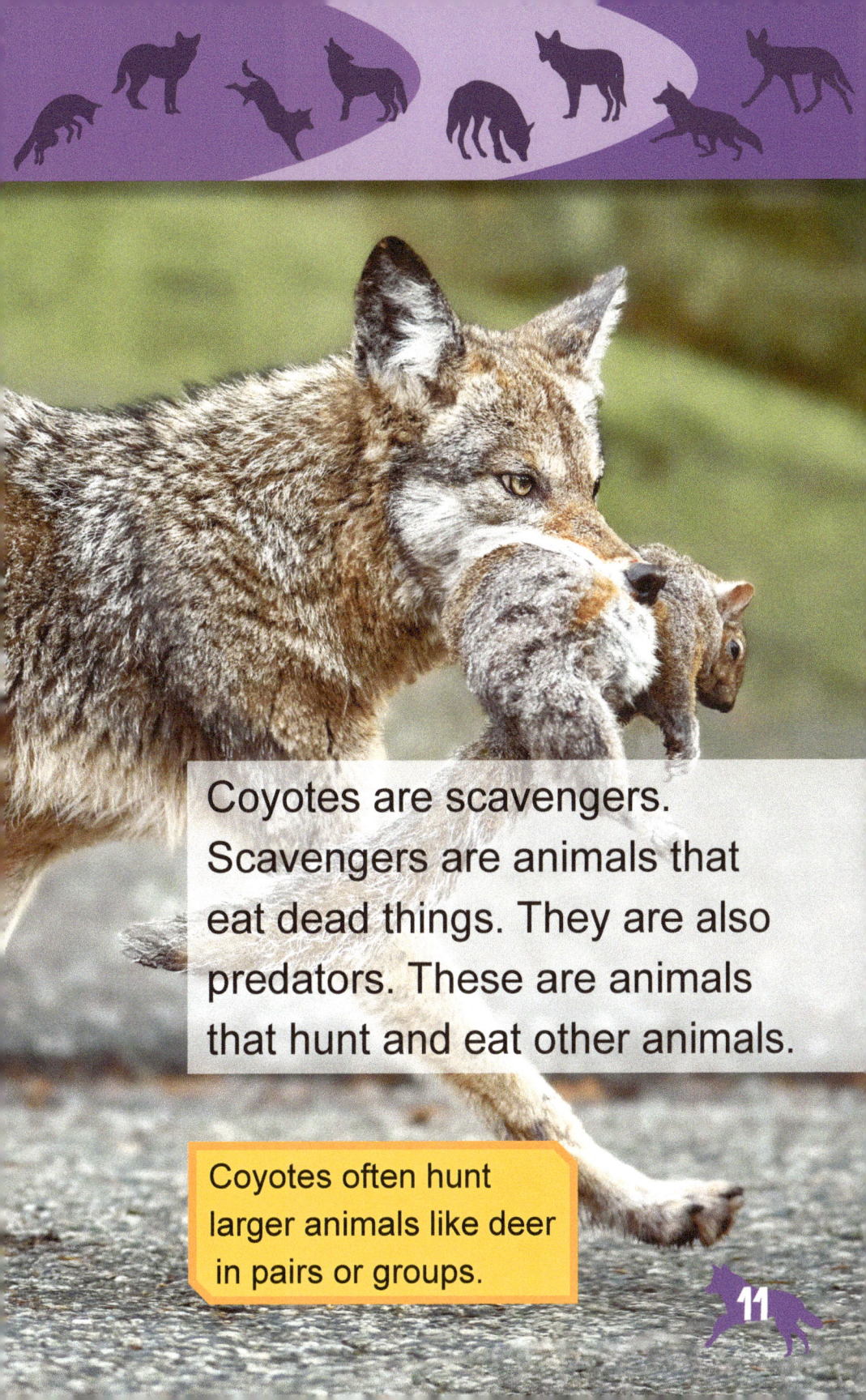

Coyotes are scavengers. Scavengers are animals that eat dead things. They are also predators. These are animals that hunt and eat other animals.

Coyotes often hunt larger animals like deer in pairs or groups.

How Do Coyotes Talk to Each Other?

Coyotes talk to each other using different sounds. They howl, bark, yelp, and huff. Coyotes howl for many different reasons. They howl to attract other coyotes or warn others to stay away from their territory.

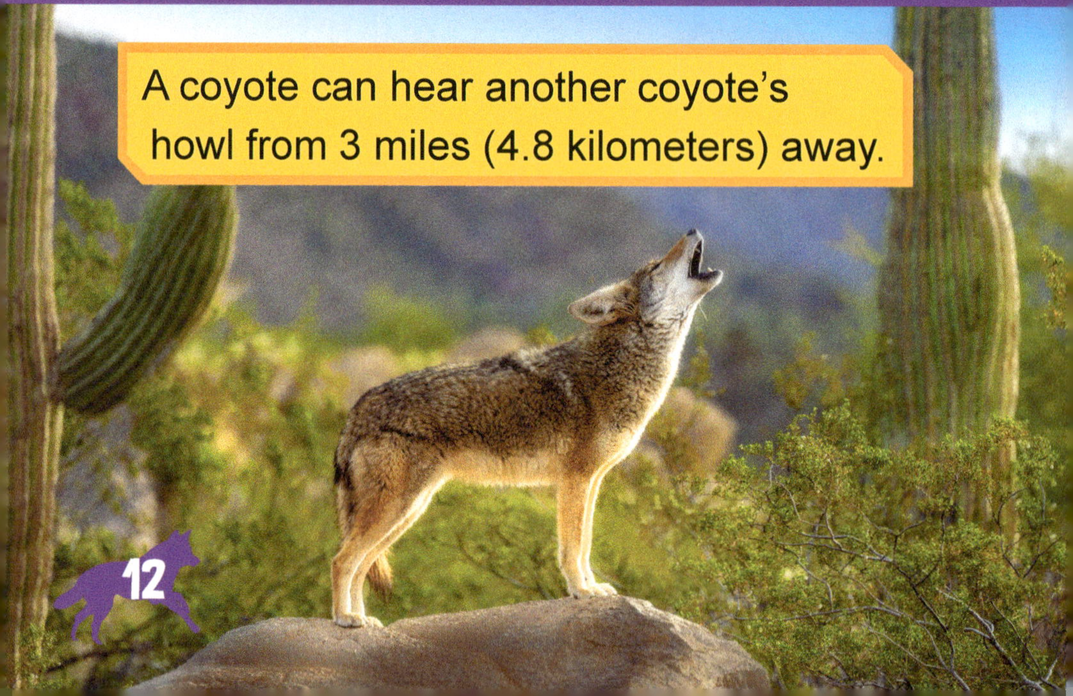

A coyote can hear another coyote's howl from 3 miles (4.8 kilometers) away.

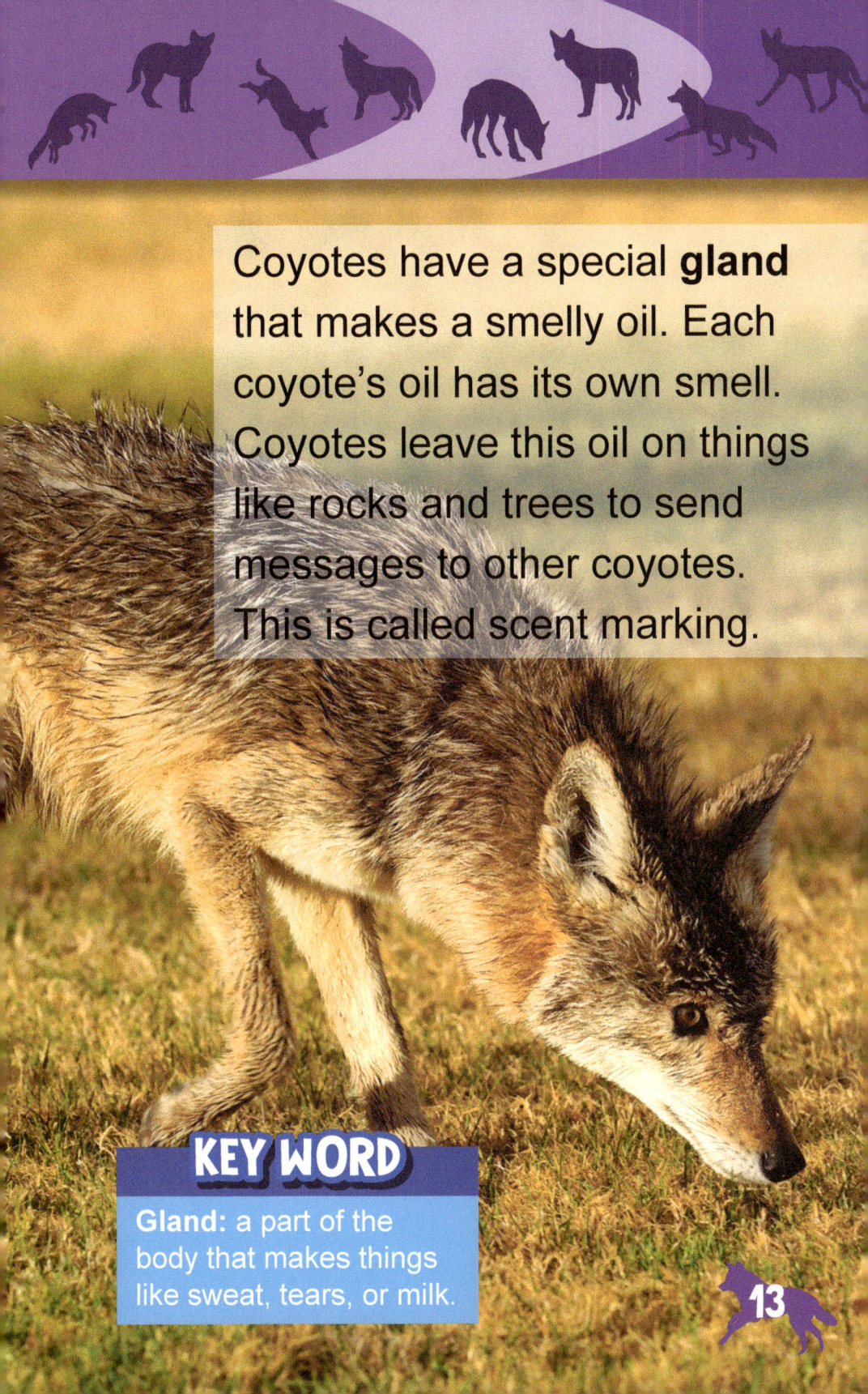

Coyotes have a special **gland** that makes a smelly oil. Each coyote's oil has its own smell. Coyotes leave this oil on things like rocks and trees to send messages to other coyotes. This is called scent marking.

KEY WORD

Gland: a part of the body that makes things like sweat, tears, or milk.

Coyote Life Cycle

Most mother coyotes will have between four and seven babies in the spring. The number of babies she has depends on how much food she can find.

Baby coyotes cannot see or hear when they are born. Older siblings often return to their home pack to help raise the new babies.

Young coyotes begin to hunt on their own in the autumn. They can live on their own within one year.

Coyotes live for 10 to 14 years in the wild. They can live for up to 20 years when kept by humans.

Curious Facts About Coyotes

Coyotes can run 40 miles (65 km) per hour.

Coyotes have 42 teeth.

Coyotes are great swimmers.

Nearly all coyotes in a pack are related.

Coyotes howl when they lose a family member.

Most adult coyotes find a partner to spend the rest of their lives with.

Kinds of Coyotes

There are 19 different kinds of coyotes. Mearns coyotes are some of the largest coyotes. They live in warm areas like Arizona and New Mexico.

Plains coyotes mostly live in grasslands. They sometimes live close to people. They have gray-brown fur and thin faces.

The bodies of California Valley coyotes are lighter in color than other coyotes. They also have larger ears than most other coyotes. They live in California's Central Valley.

How Coyotes Help Other Animals

If there are too many animals of the same kind in one place, they will eat all the food. Other animals will run out of food. Coyotes hunt whichever animal there is a lot of. This stops one kind of animal from taking over an area and eating all the food.

Foxes like to eat bird eggs and baby birds. Coyotes hunt these foxes and scare them away from their territory. This helps make sure birds do not disappear from an area.

There are more ducks in areas with coyotes than in areas with red foxes.

How Coyotes Help Earth

When coyotes scavenge food, they help break it down. This helps put important **nutrients** into the soil. These nutrients help plants and trees grow.

KEY WORD

Nutrients: things in food that help people, animals, and plants live and grow.

Deer eat a lot of plants. If there are too many deer in an area, plants start to disappear because they cannot grow back fast enough. Coyotes hunt deer and keep their numbers low. This gives plants time to grow back.

How Coyotes Help Humans

Indigenous people tell stories about how Coyote stole fire for humans. Winter had come and people were cold. Coyote felt bad for the humans. They did not have coats to keep them warm. Coyote went up into the mountains and stole fire from the fire beings. He then gave the fire to the humans.

KEY WORD

Indigenous: the first people to live in a place.

Coyotes hunt **rodents** and help keep them out of areas where people live. Hunting rodents also helps farmers. Many rodents would eat farmers' plants if coyotes did not hunt them.

KEY WORD

Rodents: small animals with long, sharp front teeth.

Coyotes in Danger

Humans are the biggest threat to coyotes. Coyote territories are destroyed as humans build more cities and farms. Farmers worry that coyotes will harm their crops or attack their farm animals. This often leads to coyotes being killed.

Diseases and **parasites** affect coyotes everywhere. Some diseases or parasites make them sick. Others can kill them. Coyotes often get diseases or parasites from eating other sick animals or animals that have been dead for a long time.

KEY WORD

Parasites: animals or plants that live on and feed on other animals or plants.

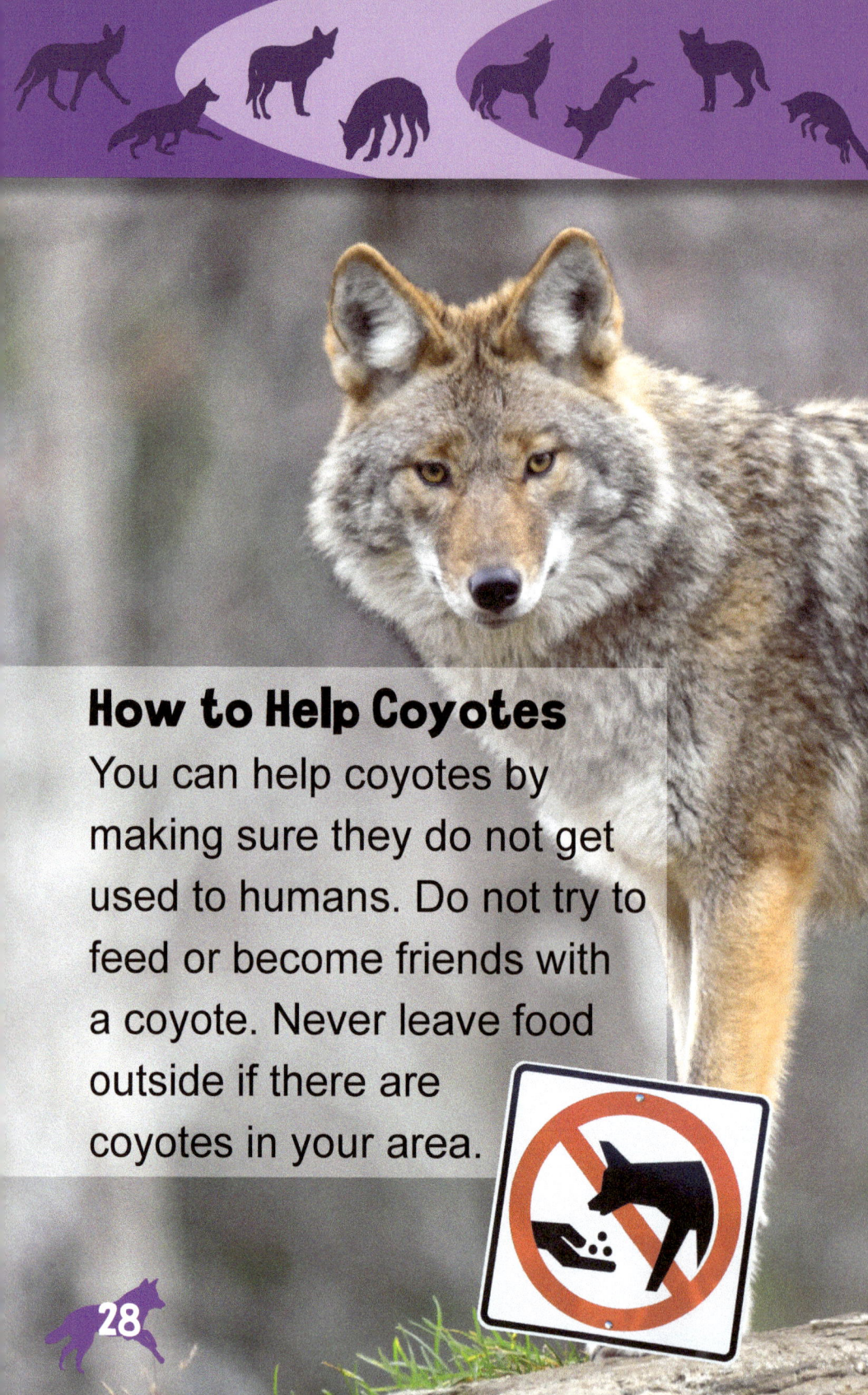

How to Help Coyotes

You can help coyotes by making sure they do not get used to humans. Do not try to feed or become friends with a coyote. Never leave food outside if there are coyotes in your area.

Do not run away if you see a coyote. It might chase you. Wave your arms and make lots of noise to scare the coyote away. This keeps you and the coyote safe.

Quiz

Test your knowledge of coyotes by answering the following questions. The questions are based on what you have read in this book. The answers are listed on the bottom of the next page.

1 What family are coyotes part of?

2 What color are coyotes' eyes?

3 Where do coyotes usually find food?

4 How many babies will a mother coyote have?

5 How many teeth do coyotes have?

6 How can you help coyotes?

Explore other books in the Animals That Make a Difference series

Visit www.engagebooks.com to explore more Engaging Readers.

Answers: 1. The dog family 2. Yellow 3. In their own territories 4. Between four and seven 5. 42 6. By making sure they do not get used to humans

Milton Keynes UK
Ingram Content Group UK Ltd.
UKHW051658081024
449373UK00018B/271